The INSIDE & OUT GUIDE to
MIGHTY MACHINES

CLINT TWIST

Heinemann
LIBRARY

CONTENTS

The INSIDE & OUT *GUIDE to*

MIGHTY MACHINES

THE INSIDE & OUT GUIDE TO MIGHTY MACHINES
was produced by

David West Children's Books
7 Princeton Court
55 Felsham Road
London SW15 1AZ

Designer: Gary Jeffrey
Illustrators: Alex Pang and Moorhen Studios
Editor: Dominique Crowley
Consultant: William Moore
Picture Research: Victoria Cook

First published in Great Britain by Heinemann
Library, Halley Court, Jordan Hill, Oxford
OX2 8EJ, part of Harcourt Education.
Heinemann is a registered trademark
of Harcourt Education Ltd.

11 10 09 08 07
10 9 8 7 6 5 4 3 2 1

10 digit ISBN: 0 431 18307 4 (hardback)
13 digit ISBN: 978 0 431 18307 7
10 digit ISBN: 0 431 18314 7 (paperback)
13 digit ISBN: 978 0 431 18314 5

British Library Cataloguing in Publication Data

Twist, Clint
Mighty Machines. - (The inside & out guides)
1. Machinery - Juvenile literature
I. Title
621.8

Printed and bound in China

PHOTO CREDITS :
Abbreviations: t-top, m-middle, b-bottom, r-right,
l-left, c-centre.

6t, Michal Wawruszak, 6b, Sierrarat; 7t, US Airforce; 8, exm
company H Goussé; 9, exm company H Goussé; 10, Blue Ai
US Airforce display team; 11t, Nicholas Koravos, 11b, US
Airforce photo; 12, Northrop Grumann; 13, NASA; 15t,
wikipedia.org, 15l, 15r, NASA; 17t, wikipedia.org, 17b, Lisa
Morris, monsterphotos.co.uk courtesy of BIGFOOT4x4 Inc;
Sparwood Chamber of Commerce, Sparwood British Colum
19, Vasko Miokovic; 20t, Frans du Plessis, 20b, Michael Ful
23, Denver Public Library, Western History Collection, 0P-
18453; 25t, 25b, US Department of Defence; 26, USS Nimit
photo lab; 27t, 27b, USS Nimitz photo lab; 29m, wikipedia.

*An explanation of difficult words can be
found in the glossary on page 30 and 31.*

INTRODUCTION

STEP INSIDE THE AWESOME WORLD OF MIGHTY machines, and meet some of the toughest vehicles on Earth. From the rugged Abrams tank to the gritty monster truck, explore their strength and brawn both inside and out. Read about the technology that allows them to haul, lift, push and pull greater loads than ever before, as see-through artwork reveals the mechanisms behind their power.

SEA KING HELICOPTER

USED IN BOTH CIVILIAN AND MILITARY AIR-SEA OPERATIONS, THE MIGHTY Sea King and its crew of five, brave all weathers to rescue people and ships in danger at sea.

The Sea King is a life-saving helicopter. Two powerful Rolls-Royce Gnome engines spin five rotor blades, which fold up neatly when not in use. The ability to hover over a single spot allows the Sea King to lower its winch and winchman to hoist casualties to safety. Sea Kings played a vital role in the December 2004 Indian Ocean tsunami relief effort, delivering supplies and saving lives.

HEAVY METAL
Massive Russian Hind helicopters have as much fire power as a tank.

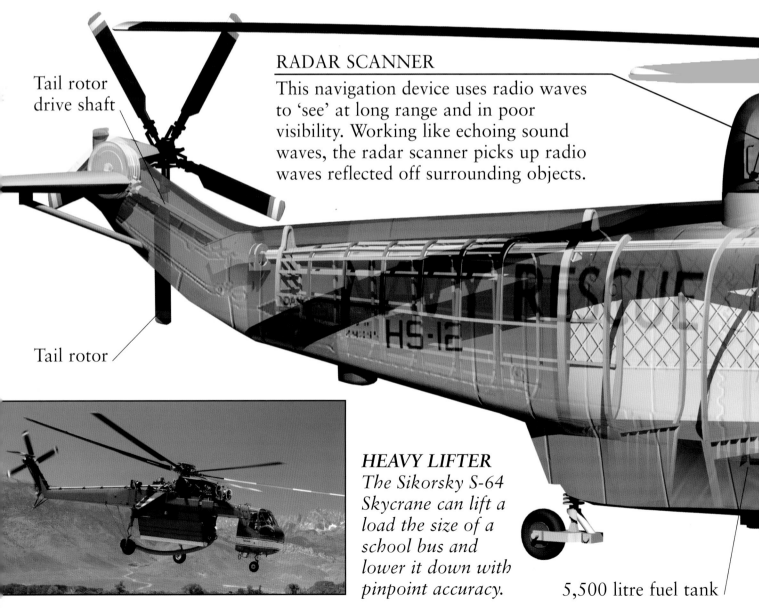

Tail rotor drive shaft

RADAR SCANNER
This navigation device uses radio waves to 'see' at long range and in poor visibility. Working like echoing sound waves, the radar scanner picks up radio waves reflected off surrounding objects.

Tail rotor

HEAVY LIFTER
The Sikorsky S-64 Skycrane can lift a load the size of a school bus and lower it down with pinpoint accuracy.

5,500 litre fuel tank

Sea Kings were originally designed to attack enemy submarines. At first, they were equipped with missiles, depth charges, and air-launched torpedoes.

HYDRAULIC WINCH
About three people, or 272 kg, can hang from the strong steel winch cable. Wind-induced swaying makes rescues hazardous. Including its crew, the Sea King can carry up to 20 people.

MAIN ROTOR
These long, flexible blades are made from a honeycomb of glass fibre and **carbon fibre**. They can withstand temperatures from –40°C to 90°C and are strengthened by a strip of titanium.

TWIN JET ENGINES
If one of its two engines fails, a Sea King can return to base, up to 510 km away from land, using the other. Sea Kings have a top speed of 250 km/h.

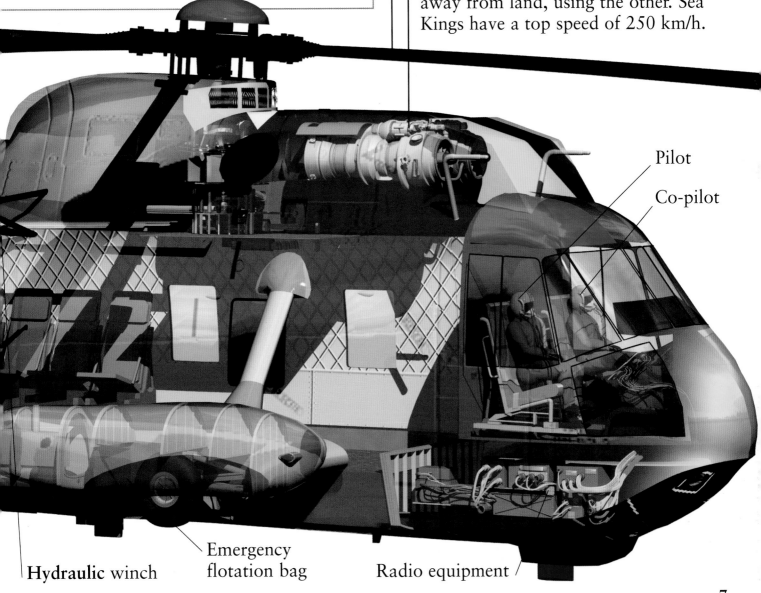

Pilot

Co-pilot

Hydraulic winch

Emergency flotation bag

Radio equipment

SUPER AIRBUS A380

THIS GIANT OF THE SKIES took fifteen years to develop. It carries 474 passengers more than a Boeing 747. The A380 storms down the runway at 272 km/h and, once airborne, will cruise at 900 km/h.

Hauling up to 555 passengers in a three-class layout or up to 880 people in a single class, the enormous A380 is the world's biggest-ever commercial airliner. When fully laden and ready for take-off it weighs an astonishing 542,000 kg – about the same as 7,000 people. Within its spacious fuselage (cabin), a relaxation room, gym, and cocktail bar transform flying. Its parts are made separately in Germany, Great Britain, Spain, and France.

AIRBORNE LUXURY
Some airlines will include shops, a dining area, and even a casino on board A380s.

FLIGHT DECK
State-of-the-art instrument panels present the crew with detailed information. An electronic **autopilot** system can land the plane automatically.

Business class

virgin atlar

Baggage hold

First class

Radar

Nose wheel

DOUBLE DECKER
Twin cabins extending along the aircraft's length accommodate 199 passengers on the upper deck and 356 on the lower deck.

Airbus claims that the environmentally friendly A380 will produce less noise and pollution than its closest competitor.

FOAM CONSTRUCTION

The fin is made of a honeycomb of plastic, reinforced by carbon fibre. It is lighter and stronger than material used on older planes.

TURBOFAN JET ENGINE

Four huge turbofan engines, mounted on struts beneath the wings, produce enormous **thrust** *(130,000 kg) to propel the A380 through the skies.*

Economy class

Engine exhaust

WING FUEL TANKS

Up to 310,000 litres of fuel is stored in long fuel tanks inside the wings. This allows the A380 to fly nearly half-way around the world without refuelling.

Control surfaces

Turbofan jet engine

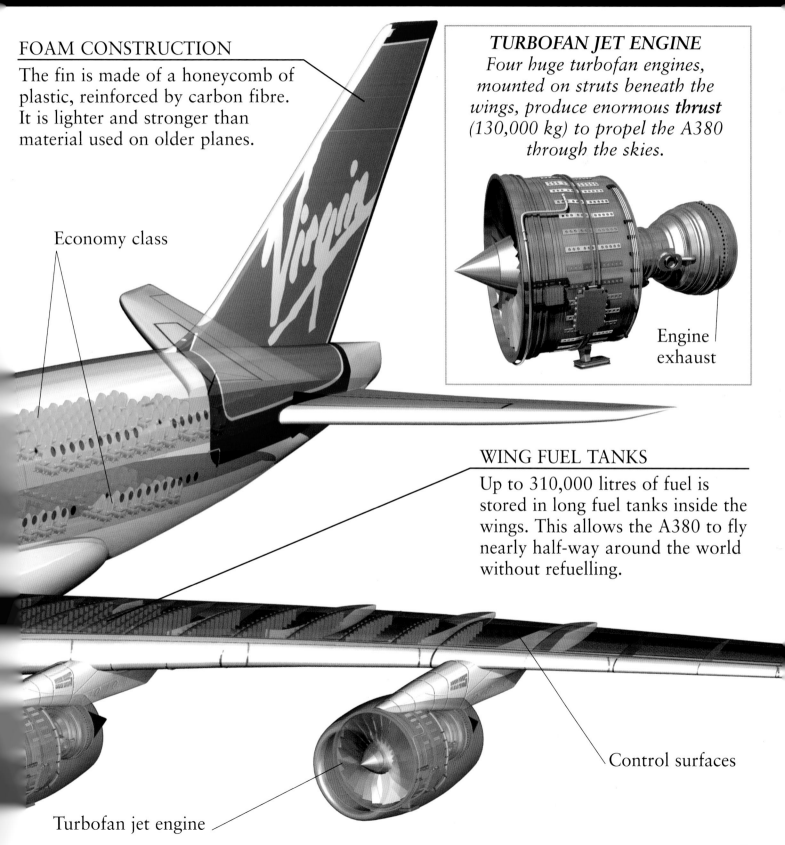

HERCULES

THIS MULTI-PURPOSE AIRCRAFT IS THE MILITARY'S most versatile transport vehicle. Whether carrying fuel for air-to-air refuelling, or flying tanks to a war zone, Hercules' fully-pressurised cavernous fuselage can hold a varied range of cargo.

Sturdy Hercules are the longest serving military aircraft, having flown for over 50 years. During this time, they have helped in civilian, military, and humanitarian aid operations. First designed in 1951 to transport 92 passengers, they are more commonly used to deliver cargo and supplies, and hold up to 61 tonnes (about 40 family cars). Access to the cargo hold is through the rear door, which can be lowered to form a full-width loading ramp. Hercules holds the world record for being the largest and heaviest plane to land on an aircraft carrier.

ROCKET BLAST-OFF
When holding super-heavy loads, Hercules are fitted with solid fuel rocket boosters. These provide extra thrust at take-off.

TURBOPROP ENGINE

Combining the power of a jet turbine (turbo) engine with the steady, long-haul performance of a **propeller** (prop) engine, the turboprop is strong, reliable, and durable.

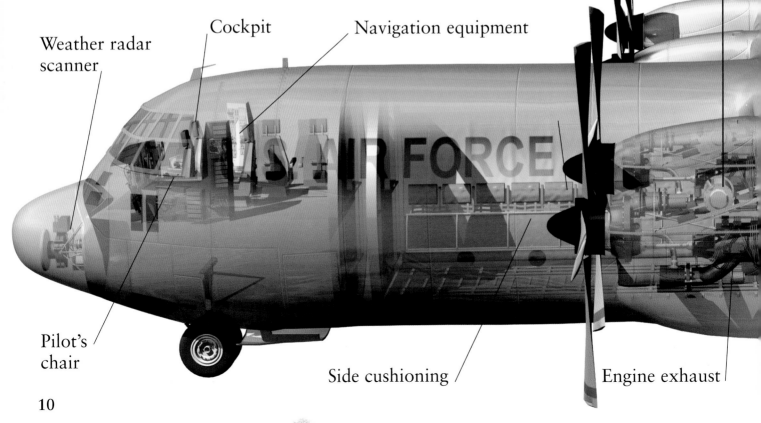

Weather radar scanner

Cockpit

Navigation equipment

AIR FORCE

Pilot's chair

Side cushioning

Engine exhaust

The Hercules is the world's most widely used STOL (short take-off and landing) aircraft. It can deliver supplies to places with short runways, or none at all.

SURFACE SKIMMING

When Hercules release their cargo without landing, they lower the rear ramp and landing gear to increase air resistance. This helps slow down the plane to prevent goods from being damaged.

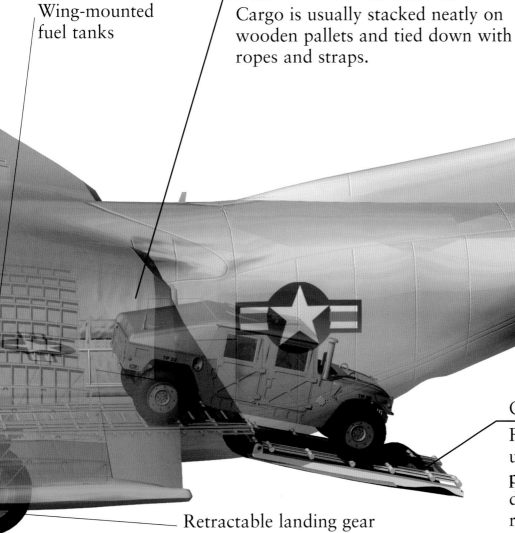

Wing-mounted
fuel tanks

CARGO HOLD

Cargo is usually stacked neatly on wooden pallets and tied down with ropes and straps.

18

CARGO RAMP

For easy loading and unloading in mid-air, a **parachute** pulls cargo down and out off the ramp at the rear.

Retractable landing gear

11

B2 BOMBER

SILENT AND DEADLY, THE B2 IS A SUPER-advanced aircraft. Its top-secret stealth technology enables it to be invisible to radar, and so drop bombs without warning. Its missions can last up to 48 hours with refuelling done in the air.

The B2 is the most costly aircraft ever developed. It would be cheaper to make it out of gold! A curved and zigzagged **bodywork** keeps it hidden from radar systems. When radar waves hit the plane, they bounce off in different directions, instead of straight back. Without the returning beams, a radar machine cannot tell there is a plane in the sky. Dark-coloured anti-radar paint also absorbs some of the waves to reduce the amount of radar reflected. Noise is muffled and heat insulated making this stealthy plane almost impossible to detect and shoot down.

LATEST MODEL
The B2 (bottom) is the latest bomber aircraft to follow the more conventional shapes of the B1 (middle) and the B52 (top).

F118-GE-100 ENGINES

Hidden on top of the wing, these special engines cool the exhaust as it leaves the aircraft. This ensures enemy systems cannot detect the B2 by using heat-detecting **infrared** devices.

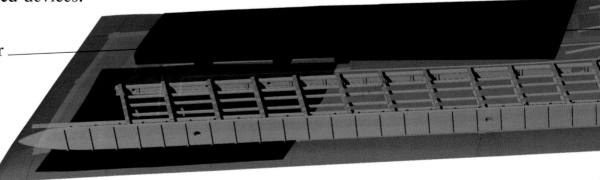

Air intake

Exhaust

Combustion chamber

Starboard outer fuel tank

The B2 has a unique 'flying wing' design – the tiny crew compartment is little more than a bump in the middle of the upper surface of the wing.

ROTARY BOMB LAUNCHER

Weapons are stowed away inside bays to prevent their detection by other military forces. A rotary launcher turns to release them one by one.

Bomb mounting clips

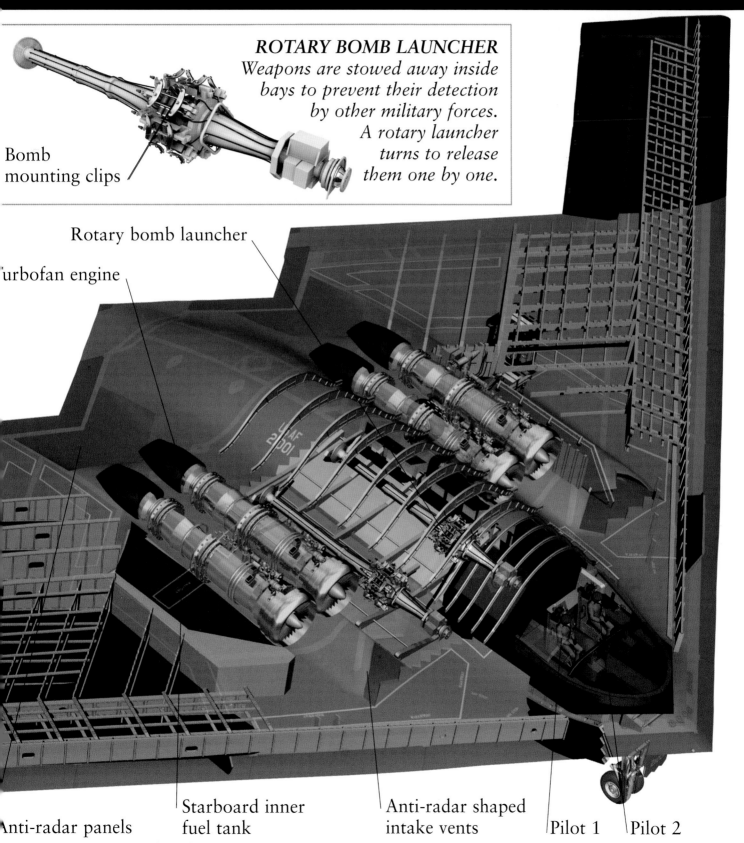

Rotary bomb launcher

Turbofan engine

Anti-radar panels

Starboard inner fuel tank

Anti-radar shaped intake vents

Pilot 1

Pilot 2

SATURN V ROCKET

Blasting off from the launch pad, this mighty rocket fired humans into their biggest adventure so far – the journey to the Moon.

Used in NASA's Apollo and Skylab programmes, the *Saturn V* is the largest of the Saturn models. It is known as a triple stage rocket because its three sets of engines are **ignited** consecutively to produce a giant force, called thrust, that shoots the rocket skywards. *Saturn V* is steered by its engines. There are five at the first stage. The middle one is fixed, and the other four turn to change the direction of travel. Once each section has burned its fuel, it is released from the rocket and falls away.

Second stage

Outer casing

First stage

Guidance fins

Saturn V rocket

OXIDISER TANK

Fuel needs oxygen to burn. In space, there is no oxygen so *Saturn V* carries its own supply in order to burn fuel and propel itself.

FUEL TANK

The first stage rocket engines use paraffin as fuel. Stages two and three use liquid hydrogen instead.

ROCKET ENGINES

Five F-1 rocket engines blast *Saturn V* from the launch pad. Fuel burns with the oxidising agent inside reaction chambers. The hot streams of exhaust gases produced send the rocket soaring into the sky.

Wernher von Braun was a brilliant German rocket scientist. Following World War II, he designed the Saturn V for the Americans and helped them to develop their space programme.

PAYLOAD SECTION

This is where the cargo is stored. It might be a spacecraft, an artificial satellite, or any number of astronauts. The payload can weigh up to twelve tonnes.

Rocket engines

Nose shroud

SKYLAB

In 1974, a Saturn V rocket launched the first space laboratory, which enabled astronauts to carry out experiments on their environment.

ALL SYSTEMS GO

Igniting on the launch pad, the first-stage F-1 engines blast the Saturn V to 8,600 km/h. They burn 2,000 tonnes of fuel.

ORBITING LAB

Skylab remained in **orbit** until 1979 when it fell back to Earth and burned up in the atmosphere.

MONSTER TRUCK

THESE AWESOME VEHICLES started life as pick-up trucks. Owners wanted to make them bigger and more powerful. An American named Bob Chandler stuck over-sized tyres on to his Ford and started driving it over scrap cars. The Bigfoot trucks were born.

Crushing smaller vehicles with four gargantuan tyres monster trucks are the ultimate entertainment machines. An ultra-strong **suspension** system allows them to leap through the air and crash back to earth without damage. A **supercharger** boosts the engine's air intake, helping the fuel to burn faster and produce more power. Occasionally, monster trucks run out of control, and hurtle towards crowds of spectators. A **remote ignition interruptor** (RII) prevents fans from being injured by cutting out the engine to stop trucks from tearing away.

Shock absorber

ENGINE

A monster truck's seven-litre V8 petrol engine provides a similar amount of power to that produced by a small tank. A **catalyst** speeds up the rate its immense engine burns fuel.

SUSPENSION

These enormous springs inside **pistons** absorb the vibrations created by landing heavily after a jump.

TYRES

Providing extra suspension, the huge tyres provide grip, helping the monster truck to clamber over **corrugated** surfaces or up steep and slippery hills.

Bigfoot is one of the biggest and most famous monster trucks. It is four metres tall, about the same in width, and weighs 10,000 kg. Each tyre is 1.8 metres in diameter, and provides extra suspension.

RECORD BREAKER

In 1999, Dan Runte set a new world record for a truck jump. His Bigfoot cleared 7.3 metres.

Exhaust

Driver's cab

Rear **axle**

BODYWORK

Strengthened bodywork and a strong steel anti-roll bar prevent the roof from caving in if the truck rolls over.

GIANT DUMP TRUCK

truck matches the amazing carrying capacity of a giant dump truck. These are too huge to be driven on public roads, and are mainly used in the construction industry, in and around mines and quarries.

Lugging and dumping tonnes of rubble, these giant transporters move loose material around construction sites. A V-shaped, reinforced tipping body is angled gently at the trucks' rear. This ensures cargo slides out easily and causes minimal damage. Giant dump trucks have a short wheelbase (the distance between the front and rear wheels), which makes them very manoeuvrable, despite their enormous size and load. The tyres are specifically designed to match a surface to reduce wear.

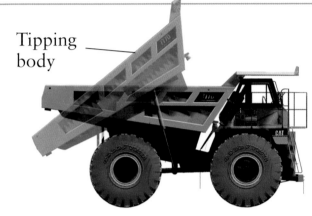

Tipping body

TIPPING POWER
The 777D delivers more than 90 tonnes of rock, the same weight as 1,000 people.

FINAL REDUCTION DRIVES
Fitted inside each wheel, these harness the power of the engine and concentrate it, to rotate the wheels steadily and slowly.

RETIRED DINOSAUR
The biggest giant dump truck ever was the Terex Titan, which could carry a load of more than 350,000 kg, the same as six Abrams tanks.

TYRES
Each of the six gigantic tyres (four at the back and two at the front) measures 2.7 metres in diameter – taller than a fully-grown man.

CATERPILLAR 777D

OFF-HIGHWAY DUMP TRUCK

A fully-laden Caterpillar 777D giant dump truck is the size of a two-storey house. Even when empty, it weighs more than 100 family cars.

Hydraulic pistons

Suspension struts

Tipping body

16-**CYLINDER DIESEL** ENGINE

With 16 cylinders, twice as many as a sports car has, the engine is super-powerful. It uses diesel instead of petrol because diesel engines have greater power to turn a wheel around an axis (torque) at lower speeds.

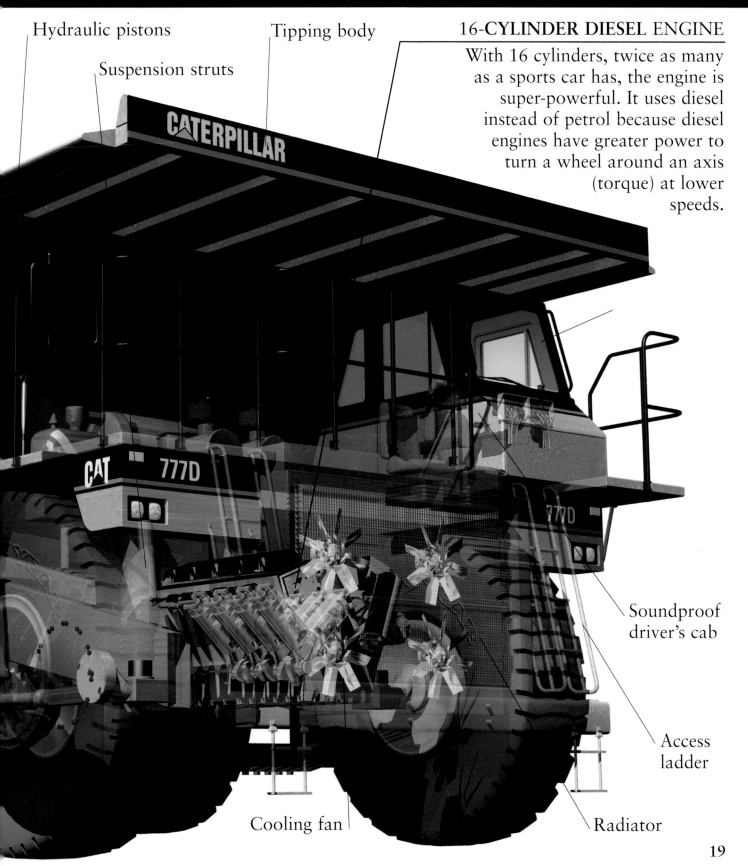

Soundproof driver's cab

Access ladder

Cooling fan

Radiator

BULLDOZER

FIGHTING FIRES AT OIL WELLS, CRASHING through woodland, or demolishing small buildings, for sheer brute force and pushing power, nothing beats a bulldozer. Like the dump truck, these are found mainly on construction sites.

Originally a tractor adapted for construction and military use, the bulldozer tears down and scoops up everything in its path. Rock, trees, and earth are shovelled in 'bull-doses' or 'giant measures' by the powerful dozer blade. Long, wide crawler tracks spread the pressure of 100 tonnes of machinery over a large area, preventing the bulldozer from sinking into soft ground. Special vehicles transport them, as they are too big to drive on roads.

SCRAPER
After the bulldozers have done the heavy work, grading machines are used to scrape the ground completely flat.

MINING SHOVEL
This giant mechanical shovel is used in opencast mines. It can rip away thousands of kilograms of rock at a time and moves at walking speed, about 5 km/h.

This bulldozer, trailing up a coal mountain, has two extra driving sprockets at its rear. These transfer more power and give the tracks a triangular shape.

HYDRAULIC RAM

Hydraulic fluid, piped into a cylinder under high pressure, moves a piston called the hydraulic ram. The ram raises and lowers the dozer blade.

Turbo diesel engine

Radiator

Engine exhaust pipe

Steering clutch

Hydraulic oil tank

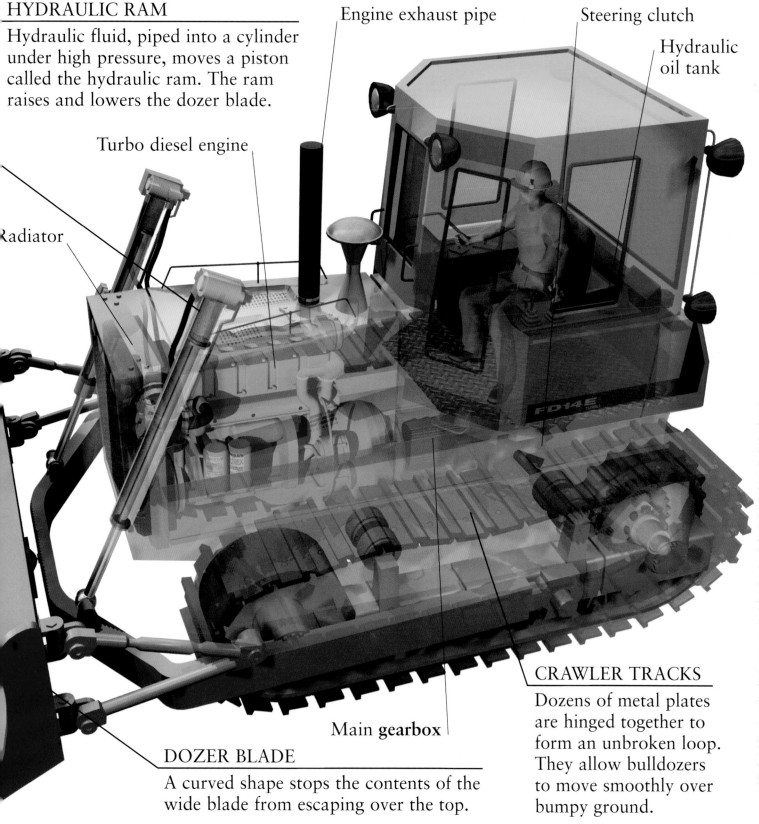

CRAWLER TRACKS

Dozens of metal plates are hinged together to form an unbroken loop. They allow bulldozers to move smoothly over bumpy ground.

Main **gearbox**

DOZER BLADE

A curved shape stops the contents of the wide blade from escaping over the top.

BIG BOY LOCOMOTIVE

the power of steam to the full, Big Boy is the largest and most powerful steam locomotive eve[r] built. It pulls heavier trains than any of its rivals, and is so long that its body must be hinged to curve around bends in the track.

Steam trains have been used for more than 150 years. They are powered by coal, which boils water to make steam. The steam is piped into cylinders that move pistons to turn wheels. Because the water is heated outside the cylinder, a steam engine is known as an external combustion engine. Petrol and diesel engines produce heat inside the cylinders, and are known as internal combustion engines. Railway locomotives can only travel up gentle slopes because their steel wheels slide on steeper tracks.

BOILER

Water, held in dozens of long, narrow tubes, is heated here to make steam. Running at 64 km/h Big Boy turns 45,000 litres of water into steam every hour.

FIREBOX

Coal is burned inside this box near the boiler. The firebox is usually made of steel or copper.

Driver's cab

TENDER

The tender is the storage area for large supplies of coal before it moves into the firebox, and water before it becomes steam.

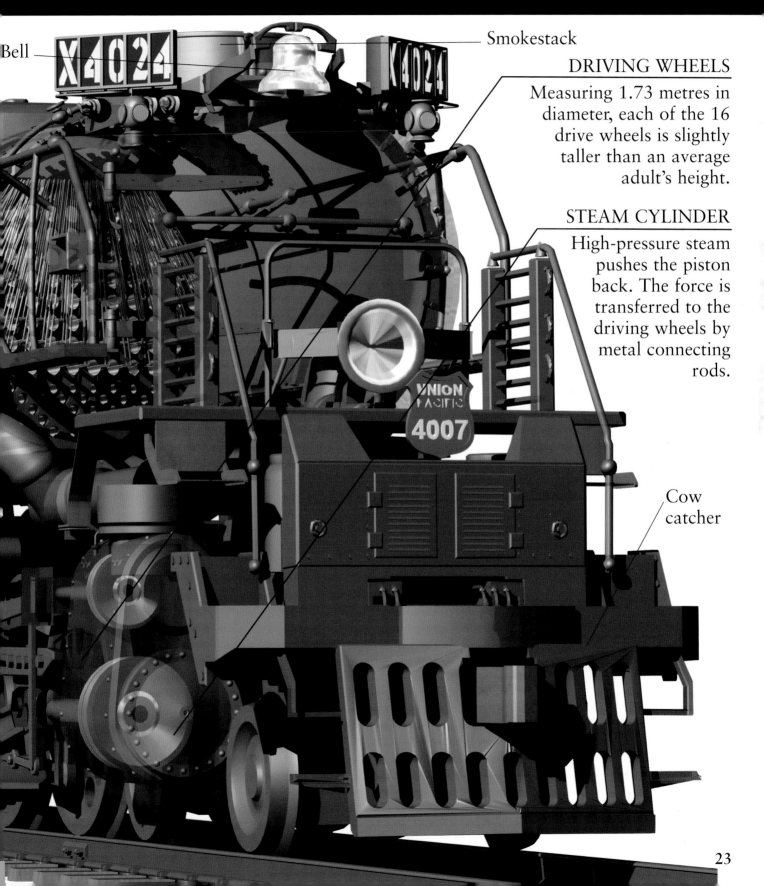

Big Boy was built to haul enormous freight trains across a mountainous region. It could pull a load of 6,000 tonnes along a slight uphill incline.

Bell

Smokestack

DRIVING WHEELS

Measuring 1.73 metres in diameter, each of the 16 drive wheels is slightly taller than an average adult's height.

STEAM CYLINDER

High-pressure steam pushes the piston back. The force is transferred to the driving wheels by metal connecting rods.

Cow catcher

4007

ABRAMS TANK

THE MOST ADVANCED TANK TO BE designed since World War II, the Abrams took more than a decade to develop. Invented in 1916, the first tank was a simple, lumbering gun platform. The Abrams has a powerful engine, excellent manoeuvrability, enormous fire power, and dense armour protection.

Weighing 62 tonnes, the Abrams is one of the heaviest tanks in the world. Yet, due to wide caterpillar tracks that spread its weight over a large area, it exerts less ground pressure per square metre than an average-sized van. The tank has weak panels above its **ammunition** and reinforced walls between its firearms and the crew. This ensures that if the tank is under fire and its ammunition ignites, it will explode away from the crew to keep them safe.

THERMAL VIEWER

Most objects produce heat. Thermal viewers sense heat and display it as a colourful image, to reveal an object even at night.

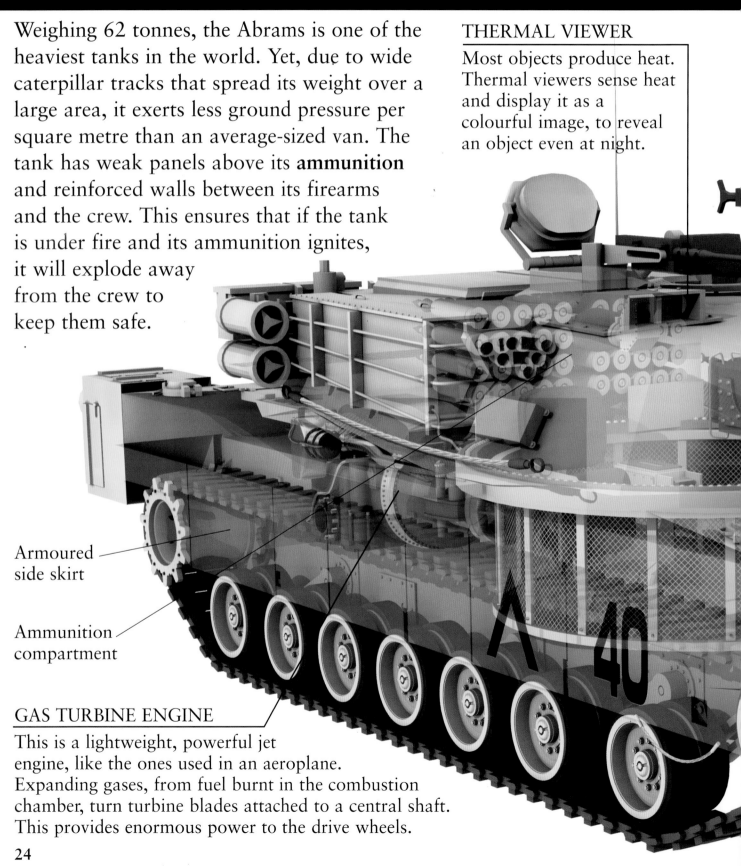

Armoured side skirt

Ammunition compartment

GAS TURBINE ENGINE

This is a lightweight, powerful jet engine, like the ones used in an aeroplane. Expanding gases, from fuel burnt in the combustion chamber, turn turbine blades attached to a central shaft. This provides enormous power to the drive wheels.

Designers made the Abrams as low as possible to make it a more difficult target. Sloping armour helps deflect bullets and shells fired by enemy tanks, protecting its four crew.

MAIN ARMOUR

Layers of metals and other materials protect the Abrams from High Explosive Anti Tank ammunition, known as HEAT rounds.

MUZZLE BLAST
Controlled explosives launch special, armour-piercing shells from the main gun, producing a bright cloud of smoke and hot gas around the gun's tip.

Smoke grenade launcher

Driver's compartment

Mudguard

Track

120 MM GUN

The Abrams fires ammunition from its main gun at speeds of over 1.6 km/s. It can destroy an enemy tank with a single shot and from more than 3 km away.

Towing lug

Driver's station

Crawler tracks

Drive wheel

THIS HUGE WARSHIP contains over 18,000 square metres of flight deck and holds 80 modern combat aircraft. Measured from the keel (the bottom of the hull) to the tip of the mast, *Nimitz* is as high as an 18-storey building.

USS Nimitz was named after Chester Nimitz, an Admiral in World War II. It carries high-speed strike aircraft that deliver bombs and rockets to distant targets. *Nimitz* also harbours jet fighters for defence against air attack, radar-equipped AWACs (early-warning aircraft), and helicopters for anti-submarine and search-and-rescue missions. Other weapons include missiles and multi-barrelled cannons. Beneath the flight decks, *Nimitz* is a small, self-contained city, criss-crossed by hundreds of passageways and staircases. Everything needed by the 5,680 crew is crammed aboard – equipment, workshops, offices, stores, kitchens, a library, a barber shop, and a fully-equipped 53-bed hospital ward.

MIGHTY POWER
When fully loaded, weighing 87,000 tonnes, four five-bladed screws (propellers) drive Nimitz *through water at speeds of up to 36 knots (nearly 70 km/h).*

Outgoing aircraft

CREW QUARTERS
Aircraft carriers operate 24 hours a day, seven days a week, and sailors work in shifts called 'watches'. At any given time about one third of them will be off-duty and asleep in their quarters.

Nimitz is powered by a pair of Westinghouse A4W nuclear reactors. It could sail around the world many times without refuelling.

Communications tower

Incoming aircraft

Ship's bridge

Loading bay

68

Propeller

ENGINE ROOM

Steam heated by the reactors is used to drive powerful turbines that turn the warship's four propellers.

Lower deck

FLIGHT DECK

The flat upper deck is divided into two side-by-side runways so that two aircraft can take off at the same time, maximising *Nimitz*'s response to an enemy attack.

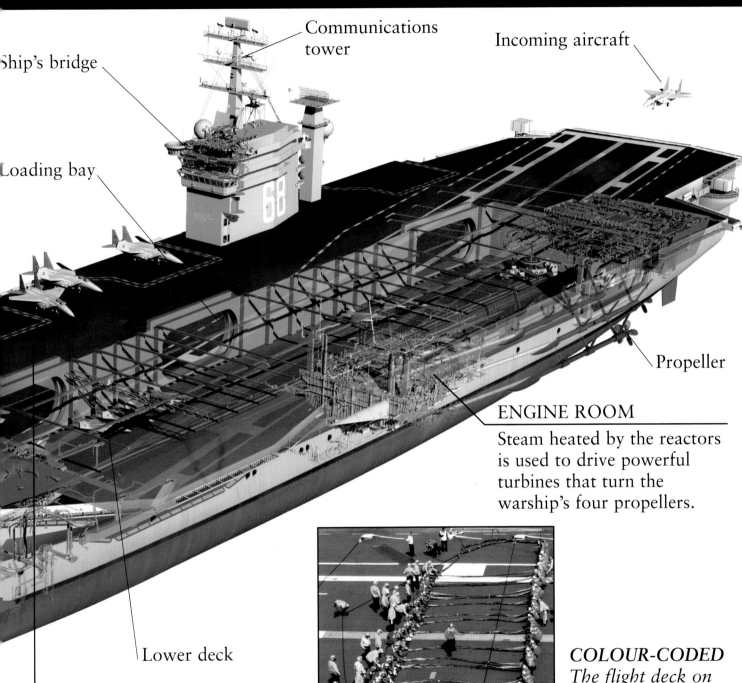

COLOUR-CODED

The flight deck on the Nimitz *can be a dangerous place. To avoid confusion, each member of the deck team is colour coded according to their role.*

TUGBOAT

FOR THEIR SIZE, TUGS ARE THE STRONGEST OF ALL boats. They are mainly used to guide ships into port, as very large vessels cannot manage small manoeuvres. The most powerful tugs can keep a damaged oil tanker afloat, or haul up a sunken ship from the seabed, and can operate in the roughest conditions.

The *Nikolay Chiker* is the world's largest and most powerful tug. It measures almost 100 metres in length and can pull up to 250 tonnes. Strong steel lines, about 20 cm in diameter, are used to tow ships. Built in Finland in 1989, the *Nikolay Chiker* is a marine salvage tug, which means that it recovers either shipwrecks or their cargo, and sometimes both. It has a small hospital on board and a helipad, while its winches contain 15 km of cable, to pull up abandoned ships from the bottom of the ocean.

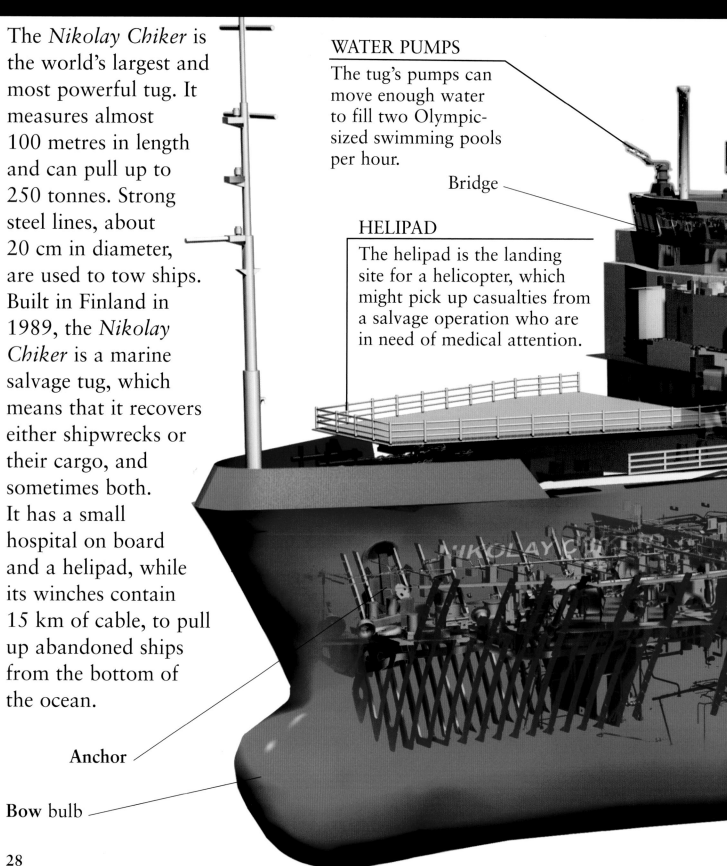

WATER PUMPS
The tug's pumps can move enough water to fill two Olympic-sized swimming pools per hour.

Bridge

HELIPAD
The helipad is the landing site for a helicopter, which might pick up casualties from a salvage operation who are in need of medical attention.

Anchor

Bow bulb

NIKOLAY CHIKER

DEEP SEA SALVAGE TUG

In a busy port, tugs are used to manoeuvre vessels in small spaces. They push against the side of the bow (front), or stern (back) to guide them to their berth.

CRANES

The *Nikolay Chiker* has three cranes, one on the starboard (right) side, and two on the **port** (left) side. They are used for hauling up objects from deep in the sea.

Crew cabins

TOWING

*Tugs can tow much larger structures than themselves, such as **oil rigs**, bridge components, and even aircraft carriers.*

Rudder

DIESEL ENGINES

Up to four high-power diesel engines drive two propellers beneath the hull. The turning propellers shoot out jets of water behind the boat to push it along.

Thick steel hull

GLOSSARY

airborne
Flying in the air.

ammunition
The bombs, shells, and bullets fired from a weapon.

anchor
A heavy piece of metal with hooks, attached to a ship by a long metal chain. It catches on to objects on the seabed to keep a ship stationary.

autopilot
Short for automatic pilot, this machine steers the plane on a preset course.

axle
A rod on which a wheel turns.

berth
The place where a boat moors.

bodywork
The outer shell of a vehicle.

bow
The front of a boat.

carbon fibre
A strong, light material that is used in aeroplanes and racing cars. It can be more than twice as stiff as steel.

catalyst
A substance that speeds up a chemical reaction without being changed.

civilian
Any person who is not a member of the armed forces or police.

corrugated
A surface made of a series of folded bumps, called ridges.

cylinder
The metal sleeve inside which a piston moves.

diesel
A type of fuel that burns when it is squashed, named after inventor Rudolph Diesel.

gearbox
The box containing gears that transfer power from the engine to the wheels.

hydraulic
Something that works by the pressure of water or another liquid in pipes.

ignite
To set fire to.

infrared
Radiation just beyond red in the visible spectrum. It is usually felt as heat.

nuclear reactor
A device that produces nuclear energy. Nuclear energy is the energy that exists in the centre of tiny particles, called atoms.

oil rig
The structure, machinery, and drilling equipment that are used to drill for oil.

orbit
A circular path around a body in space, such as the Earth.

parachute
A loose umbrella of light fabric used to slow things down in air.

piston
A cylinder that moves to and fro within another cylinder.

port
The term used to describe the left of a ship or aircraft.

propeller
A device with a number of angled blades that spins to push water or air in a particular direction to move a boat through water or a plane through air.

remote ignition interruptor
The RII enables an engine to be switched off from outside a vehicle.

sprocket
A wheel with a set of teeth around its rim.

starboard
The term used to describe the right of a ship or aircraft.

stealth
Secretive and avoiding notice.

supercharger
A pump that helps an engine to take in more air and so in turn burn more fuel.

suspension
A system of shock absorbers and springs that cushions the vibrations sent from a road surface to a vehicle.

tender
A railway carriage that carries fuel and water as part of a steam train.

thrust
The force produced by a jet or rocket engine that sends it forwards.

INDEX